W9-BDX-144

GOOPS & LETTERS

Coloring Book

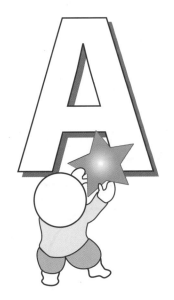

Illustrations by Janie Berry

Goops Unlimited
© 2010
P.O. Box 1840
Battle Ground, WA 98604
www.TheGoops.com

Alligator

Aa

A

Print my letter _____

Colored by _____

Bear

B b

Print my letter _____

Colored by _____

Print my letter _____

Colored by _____

Donkey

D d

Print my letter _____

Colored by _____

Elephant
Ee

Print my letter _____

Colored by _____

Print my letter _____

Colored by _____

Giraffe
Gg

Print my letter _____

Colored by _____

Horse

Print my letter _____

Colored by _____

Iguana

I i

Print my letter _____

Colored by _____

Jaguar

Jj

Print my letter_____

Colored by_____

Kangaroo

K k

Print my letter _____

Colored by _____

Print my letter _____

Colored by _____

Print my letter_____

Colored by_____

Nightingale

Nn

Print my letter _____

Colored by _____

Ostrich

O o

Print my letter _____

Colored by _____

Pig

p

P

p

Print my letter _____

Colored by _____

Quaesitosaurus

Q q

Print my letter _____

Colored by _____

Raccoon

Rr

Print my letter _____

Colored by _____

Seal Ss

Print my letter _____

Colored by _____

Turtle
T t

Print my letter＿＿＿＿＿＿＿＿＿＿＿＿＿＿＿＿＿＿

Colored by＿＿＿＿＿＿＿＿＿＿＿＿＿＿＿＿＿＿

Utahraptor
Uu

Print my letter _____

Colored by _____

Vinegarroon

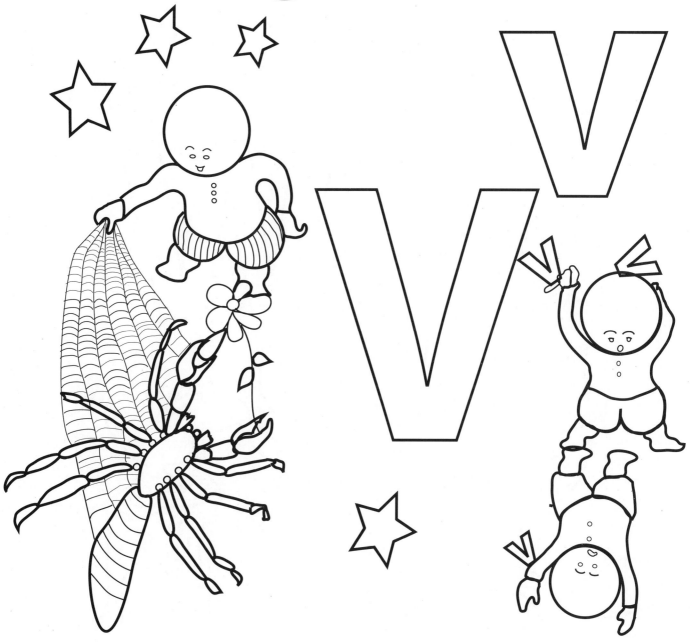

Print my letter _____

Colored by _____

Woodchuck

W
W

Print my letter _____

Colored by _____

Xenops

Print my letter _____

Colored by _____

Print my letter _____

Colored by _____

Zebra

Print my letter _____

Colored by _____

Practice Your Letters Here

A _____

a _____

B _____

b _____

C _____

c _____

D _____

d _____

E _____

e _____

Practice Your Letters Here

F _____

f _____

G _____

g _____

H _____

h _____

I _____

i _____

J _____

j _____

Practice Your Letters Here

K _____

k _____

L _____

l _____

M _____

m _____

N _____

n _____

O _____

o _____

Practice Your Letters Here

P _____

p _____

Q _____

q _____

R _____

r _____

S _____

s _____

T _____

t _____

Practice Your Letters Here

U _____

u _____

V _____

v _____

W _____

w _____

X _____

x _____

Y _____

y _____

Z _____

z _____